How To Write Short Romance

The Quick and Easy Guide to Writing Instalove

Nell Alexander

Copyright © 2022 Nell Alexander All rights reserved

No part of this book may be reproduced, or stored in a retrieval system, or transmitted in any form or by any means, electronic, mechanical, photocopying, recording, or otherwise, without express written permission of the publisher.

ISBN-13: 978-1-8381782-2-2

Introduction

As I'm sat here writing this, Autumn 2022 is well underway. It's a time of year I use to reflect, before the chaos of Christmas and New Year take over.

What am I reflecting on this year?

The rise of Short Romance.

Slowly but surely it's become a booming space full of voracious readers, and in comparison to full-length romance, seems vastly underserved.

What is Short Romance? It's a full short story, in the romance genre, encompassing any tropes or sub-genres, and it can usually be read in a lunch break.

So popular have short reads become, that Amazon launched the short-read categories for Kindle (more on those later).

And what are we writers hearing more and more in our reviews?

'Engrossing short story.' – The Birthday Boyfriend

'A very quick and very well written mountain man romance.' – Ink For The Mountain Man

'This is a quick read, but very enjoyable.' - Colt

I decided to write this book after providing a plan, for lack of a better term, to people who wanted to give short romance a go. A lot of new and aspiring writers seem to think that by starting their career by writing short romances, they can learn the ropes of indie publishing and how to write a successful romance all in one fell swoop. But as with anything in life, it's never that simple.

This book is written specifically so you can try and avoid the pitfalls that many an indie romance writer falls into, by not making the same mistakes I did. And the first mistake? Believing that writing short romance is easy.

Because it isn't.

That's not to put you off, but you must remember that you are trying to cram something that would usually develop over 50-75,000 words into a short story of between 7-20,000 words.

That is no mean feat. The beats* are different for Short Romance. And trust me when I've said I've read most of them, and there are a lot of them.

I'm going to show you how and what to do to get your first short romance series written. I won't be going into tremendous detail on formatting or uploading etc, because there's tons of info on that readily available for free online. I also won't be going into huge detail about marketing in this book, just those I know well from my own experience.

Finally, thank you for giving this book a read, and I

hope you find it to be useful.

*Beats are the notes or points you need to hit at sometimes very specific times within your story. Check out Gwen Hayes' Romancing The Beat for more information on beats within full length romance.

What Short Romance Is, And Isn't

Short romance is like full-length romance only shorter. It sounds simple but sometimes you may find it's anything but.

A romance is defined by several key factors. It must have a Happily Ever After (referred to as HEA) for the main characters, or a Happy For Now (HFN) if the story is going to continue over several books. There can be no cheating. You may find in some reviews where reader is calling a book "safe," and even some blurbs may refer to the books as a "safe romance." This means that once the main characters have met, they aren't ever with anyone else again. Romance also means that it's the relationship between the couple that pushes the story forward.

If you find you want to write steamy romance but that the couple never gets dressed and that it's their sexual connection that's pushing the story forward, then that's probably erotica.

If you find your story doesn't have the elements mentioned above, you might be writing in a different genre. Possibly women's fiction, or even a thriller that has a romantic element. Which is great, but not what this book is here to help with.

To recap, you want to write a Short Romance that tells a complete story between a couple who only have eyes for each other and ends with a Happily Ever After or Happy For Now.

And in that story, you need to make it enticing and exciting for the reader by having tons of conflict and angst.

But how can you do that in as few as 7,000 words?

The beats for Short Romance are different because you do not have the word count to do it all. Which is why the term Instalove will become your bedrock.

Think about your favourite romance novel. Who wrote it? How long is it? How did it start? How did it end? Who else was introduced to help move the story forward?

Now imagine fitting all that into a Short Romance. It's just not possible. You need to pick the most vital elements and use those. This is as important to the readers as it is to you as the writer. If the reader leaves reviews like "nothing really happened" or "things jumped around too much without any explanation," then you've missed the mark.

I've missed the mark in a few of my backlist books and I'm eager to go back and change them, but then other Short Romance authors have done the same and I've learned to have respect for those dodgy earlier releases. It's how I cut my teeth. It's how I developed a story writing strategy that works.

The magic here is that you get to choose your word count based on what you're comfortable with (which you'll learn once you start writing them regularly) and what you want to set your reader expectations at. You might find that you want to write super steamy romance, and I can assure you, a short sex scene can run you a thousand words easily, especially when told from two points of view.

Grab yourself a notebook and make a few notes about what you want to write in more detail. Steam levels are discussed all over the internet but my books are usually classed as lighter steam and I usually have two intimate scenes (this means either oral sex or penetrative sex on the page, doors wide open).

Jot down what tropes you love, enemies to lovers? Friends to lovers? Forced Proximity? Then take a look at the following chapter...

Short Romance Beats

The following is what I've gleaned from reading all of those successful and amazing authors who write Short Romance. These aren't set in stone. You may want the ***First Kiss*** to always happen at the 25% mark in your story. That's fine. Put it there. Once you get the basic maths of your word count, you'll know where and when you need to hit the beats.

These are the beats I use to write my romance, and this seems to be the most used flow. Now, you're going to think to yourself "I don't want my books to be like everyone else's!" and that's fine. You do you. But trust me when I say, there's a reason that things are done in a certain way.

1. Intro to Heroine/Hero
2. Intro to Hero/Heroine
3. Meet Cute
4. Growing attraction/Getting to know each other
5. First Kiss (first spark/contact if you're writing Clean Romance)
6. Internal conflict/Resistance to attraction

7. Intimate scene (this can be Clean or Steamy)
8. Internal falling in love
9. Dark moment/Pulling apart
10. Resolution
11. Happily Ever After

If you don't want to do them in this order. That's okay. Some of them can't be moved, for example, you're going to want to introduce at least one of your characters at that first beat. You might want your first kiss to happen right before they have their first sexual contact (I've done this too, and it works for some characters), you might not want them to have their intimate beat until the very last chapter.

What I find helps me is writing each beat on an index card or post-it note and sticking it on my wall, then I'll move them around with my characters in mind and see what works.

Nothing is set in stone, that's the beauty of it. Experiment, feel your way through your writing and do what makes you happy. Because there's one thing I know for certain, if you don't love what you're doing, you won't be able to keep doing it!

There's no rush. The Short Romance genre still has a lot of room for growth and I promise you aren't going to miss the boat if you spend a few extra hours figuring out what feels good for you in terms of your characters and your story structure.

Instalove Series

The Short Romance community has lovingly coined the term **instalove**. Sometimes used by readers of longer fiction in a derogatory or negative way to review someone's work, because instalove is largely unrealistic. The first thing you need to come to terms with as a writer of short romance is that instalove is going to be real in your world. It has to be.

Why?

Word count.

There is no room to lay down a huge backstory or a foundation of angst. To have the constant push and pull that a novel requires to move the relationship forward. You'll also find that there's no room to add a huge catalogue of side characters. But that's why working in a series will benefit you. Your first book will introduce enough of a background for the other characters to make sense when they arrive on scene in their own stories.

Here's an example from my own backlist:

My Mountain Heroes series takes place on Montrossi

Ridge, a fictional small town at the foot of a mountain. The first book introduces Aiden and Molly. We learn Aiden works for the mountain rescue team and we meet a couple of the other people from that team.

That's it!

There's no room for anything else...*in that book*. But that's where the fun begins because it leads your readers to the next book, the next adventure, the next love story.

In Tilly's Mountain hero (book two) we meet Ford and again, see a few of the others in passing, plus have snippets from Molly and Aiden's life now, such as the fact that Molly's sister is in town (character for later on). These snippets add up in your readers' minds and you'll be surprised how much they remember!

Which reminds me...

I highly recommend sticking to one series at a time.

You're not just writing in a series to group all your characters together and to create multiple love stories within one world, or to make it easier for readers to pick up your next book for the sake of it. It's to hook your readers with the first book and keep them engaged and invested. Because those readers who are choosing to read the next book, and the next, is how you will earn money through your writing. So, the sooner you get the series completed and introduce the next, the easier it is to keep your readers hooked on your books.

I recently read a review where the reader didn't enjoy the book. But they took the time to mention that they were still going to read through that authors entire backlist, and I'm talking seventy-plus books! They are the readers you want to hook. The ones who will give you a second chance when you mess something up.

An example of something I did that messed something up. I write low-steam, pretty vanilla sex scenes. At the urging of my critique partner, I spiced things up in Colt with a bit of light spanking. My readers HATED it with such passion I've never even dipped a toe into that level of steam ever again.

And back to talking about writing in a series…this year (2022) I decided I didn't want to write an entire series back-to-back. Oh no! I thought I'll spice up my life a little by dipping in and out of the different series' I was writing (three of them) as and when I fancy it.

THIS WAS A HUGE MISTAKE.

Now I have to remove myself from one world and place myself into another each time I sit down to write. It is not fun. However, if your brain can handle that (and some people can handle that amazingly well) then go for it. Find what works for you. But remember, you're writing for the readers. They might not like you dipping in and out of series' either. My readers don't. And I've paid a heavy price for that financially.

I went off on a tangent there. But essentially, your

short romance will have to be INSTALOVE because you don't have the word count to make it a slow burn.

And remember, this is fiction. It is allowed to be unrealistic as long as it's within the realms of the expectations YOU set for your readers.

Create your own world with its own rules and anything is possible.

Writing in a Series

First and foremost, this is a marketing strategy.

If readers pick up your first book in a series and love it, they are more likely to read the next in that series. The next in series information should always be immediately available in the backmatter, along with a link. The amazing Zoe York once recommended to me to have the purchase link for the next in the series, then the excerpt (I use the first chapter from the next book) then the purchase link again. There's an example of this under the "Backmatter" heading in this book.

How long should a series be?

That's completely up to you. I wanted to do a series of six books and a boxset, but I found that I got bored of the series by the end of book five, so I only write five book series' now. Then there's the case of a series not doing well, like my Rugged Coast series. I stopped writing those after book three but have not yet released the boxset in case I decide to add more later. The Flower Market series is also only four books but that's because I only ever planned it to be four books. There was going to be a spin-off series of six books that I never got around to writing.

The other thing about series is that while you may only want to write a specific amount, say four books, it doesn't mean that they can't be in the same world. I've not got two series based in the same world (Montrossi Ridge) and I'll be adding another. This enables me to firstly, not get bored of the characters, and secondly, be able to link the books together across series' to keep readers reading!

Series Plan

I do recommend creating a series plan. If the thought of having a strict plan freaks you out (it does me) then consider it a loose guidance, because that's all it is until you find where you fit.

Here's a series plan example:

> Series Title: *The Wild Brothers.*
>
> Books in Series: *Five; One for each brother.*
>
> Tropes: *Second Chance Romance, Mountain Man.*
>
> Book Word Count: *10k.*

That's it. Maybe give this a go in your notebook and see if your creative juices start flowing. Here's an example of one of my (as yet unfinished) series plans.

> Series Title: *Mountain Heroes (Men Of Montrossi Ridge)*
>
> Books in Series: *Five; One for each member of the mountain rescue team.*
>
> Tropes: *Mountain Man, Damsel In Distress.*
>
> Book Word Count: *10k.*

It might be that you find you want to write trilogies, or even standalones not in a series at all.

Again, that's fine.

Just make sure you send your readers to your next book (or another of your books) in your backmatter. That way they'll always have the read just a click away.

Standalones are possibly a quicker way to build up your backlist if the idea of a four-plus book series feels too daunting to you right now. You'll learn what works for you as you go, and be able to adapt accordingly.

That's the other amazing thing about being an indie author. You don't have other people breathing down your neck to do a certain thing a certain way.

But remember, readers do have expectations. So, if you've promised them four books in a series, deliver four books. If you've promised six but you can see the series is a flop at three (a la my Rugged Coast series), you can stop writing at three. But really that's the only time it's okay to cut a series short unless you want to get ready to deal with a few disgruntled readers, who in future, might not want to read a series you write until it's completed.

The next step in the Series Plan is Titles.

Book 1: *Molly's Mountain Hero*

Book 2: *Tilly's Mountain Hero*

Book 3: *Bette's Mountain Hero*

Book 4: *Cora's Mountain Hero*

Book 5: *Abbie's Mountain Hero*

You can change these (I just did, I changed Leah to Abbie because I've already mentioned Abbie in Book 3). You're in charge, remember?

Then you can brainstorm some ideas about the setting (a series usually shares a setting, like Montrossi Ridge is the setting for this series) and characters.

Now you can go ahead and write a synopsis or blurb for each book if you want to. Personally, I don't do this as it's too much like planning and I am a pantser through and through.

However, I would recommend a few notes around tropes or specific types of characters in case you come back to your series plan and realise you don't remember anything about the ideas you had at the time. I've got so many pieces of paper lying around with series plans and yet I cannot remember what inspired me at the time and the passion I knew I had for a series is hard to find when I've nothing to trigger the memory. That might just be me. But either way, a couple of sentences won't hurt even if they change later on.

Framework

I use a pretty strict word count framework for my writing, it doesn't matter if I go over or under, as long as it's not by much. This is for a couple of reasons; I might want to hit a specific short category.

a) ***I might want to hit a specific short-reads category***.

Consider the time it takes to read your short romance. Usually, 12-21 pages equate to thirty-minute reads, 22-32 pages is a forty-five-minute, 33-43 is a one-hour read and 44-64 is a ninety-minute read. Depending on how long your story is, is where your book will be categorised on Amazon, which has a whole set of advantages of its own.

Your page count doesn't just depend on your word count but also on how you format your story.

Here are examples using my books;

Family for the Mountain Man. The word count before backmatter is 6630. Amazon has the page count listed as 52 which puts it in the ninety-minute read category.

Curves for the mountain man is 7829 words before backmatter. Amazon has the page count listed at 58 and it's therefore still in the 90-minute read category.

You can manipulate your page count through formatting and reducing front and backmatter. But Amazon does change these categories with the more information they get. Therefore, this information is subject to change from time to time.

b) ***I might want that specific series to touch on certain subjects that might need a few more words.***

My Rugged Coast series (which happens to be my worst performing series) were all books that touched on serious and upsetting issues such as; domestic violence, a parent with dementia and a single mum with a potential custody battle on her hands. Pro-tip, readers don't want this in their short romance. So, if you have a hankering to write a serious thread through your short romance, **don't**.

Save it for your novels.

You always have the option of teasing this in your series and then link a full-length novel at the back of your book IF there are readers that would be interested in reading that story. That way you have the added advantage of making the readers care about these characters enough for them to consider buying a book they never intended on reading in the first place.

I'm going to provide the framework for 7k, 10k, 15k and 20k word novels. I started out as a big advocate of the 7k short story as these were always my better-selling series'. However, I've found lately I can't stop writing and usually finish between 10k and 15k.

You will find what works for you with your own writing style and voice. But feel free to use any of these as a guide.

Chapter	Beat	7k	10k	15k	20k
Prologue		150	300	300	500
Chapter One	Intro to FMC	450	700	1000	1250
	Intro to MMC	450	700	1000	1250
Chapter Two	Meet Cute	750	1100	1400	2500
Chapter Three	Getting to know each other	900	1100	2300	3000
	First Kiss	400	550	1000	1000
Chapter Four	Internal Conflict	500	1000	1200	1500

Chapter Five	Intimacy	700	1200	1400	2000
	Falling In Love	500	700	1200	1500
Chapter Six	Dark Moment	1000	1000	1500	2000
Chapter Seven	Resolution	500	600	1200	1500
Chapter Eight	Happily Ever After	550	750	1200	1500
Epilogue		150	300	300	500

Writing Speed

To figure out your writing speed, sit down for an uninterrupted twenty-minute writing sprint and see how many words you get down.

Now, this will be different for everyone and will depend on different personality traits. One course I wholeheartedly recommend you do is Becca Syme's Write Better Faster (I'm not affiliated, I just loved it *that* much).

This course will essentially tell you your personality type and why you can't do things a certain way, and why, more importantly, you can do them *other* ways.

A brief example (you can skip this if you want).

My DISC (Jungian) score puts me at Stability 94%. This means if my personal life doesn't feel stable to me – I cannot write.

It's as simple (and as complex) as that.

The course goes into detail for several tests and personality types and has changed a lot of people's lives; mine included. I no longer beat myself up when I struggle to get the words down; I now know that sprinting (also known as the Pomodoro

Technique) is the only way I get the words down. But to do that successfully I need other stuff in place.

Anyway, back to figuring out your average writing speed.

Once you've written uninterruptedly for twenty minutes and taken a ten-minute break between sprints, multiply that number by two. Technically, all being well, that's your hourly average.

This is what it looked like for me when I first started sprinting last year (remember, everyone is different, and whatever your number is here, it is the right number for you!)

20 minutes of writing (ten-minute break) = 750 words.

Multiplied by two (because there are two thirty-minute blocks in an hour)= 1500 words.

1500 words per hour if I work in twenty-minute sprints with ten-minute breaks.

You might have more, or you might have less. You might find that you work better in shorter or longer sprints with shorter or longer breaks. Whatever works for you is the best way for you to work!

Now determine how long you want your books to be. Maybe ignore the above framework and write to your heart's content following the short romance beats. See what happens. You may find that you hit the beats in a readable and workable manner in 12k words (which falls between my examples above) that's okay. You know your average short romance (because you've only written the one) is 12k words.

Now divide 12000 by your average hourly word count and that will tell you how long it will take you (roughly) to write your short romances.

Let's say you average 2000 words per hour comfortably; 12000/2000 = 6.

Six hours to write one entire short romance.

So how many hours a day can you write? I get up at 4.30am and have two hours of uninterrupted writing a day. However long you have, thirty minutes or four hours, multiply that by your words to find your daily average.

Two hours of writing at 2000 words per hour = 4000 words per day.

Then 12000/4000 = 3

Now you know that it will take you six hours over three days to complete a short romance on approximately 12000 words.

There is a caveat here.

As I mentioned above, if I'm having personal life issues I cannot write. It doesn't matter how long I stare at my manuscript. If you find that you aren't writing as quickly as whatever your normal is, it's okay. Take a break, refill the well, spend time with family and friends or treat yourself to something you enjoy and helps you to relax. Then come back and try again.

The Seed of an Idea

Okay, you know there are plotters and pantsers and everything in between. I am not a plotter, however, I need an idea before I can start to write. If I don't have an idea the series doesn't get written at all. I can usually scribble out an idea while I'm doing a series plan, but I keep it loosy-goosy so I can go off on my tangents.

If you are a plotter you can use each beat as a heading and write a couple of sentences to help the flow of your writing when you're in the zone. Sometimes I do this, and force myself to stick to it. I usually don't like how the story goes. Raife, was one such example and my first ever short romance, so it doesn't follow the beats accurately at all, but then the readers mostly like it, so it's a win, right?

However you prefer to write, whether it's with a firm outline or seeing where your characters take you, make it work for you. Keep your writing tight by following the framework for word counts otherwise you might find you go off on a tangent and end up needing to delete a load of words. That is disheartening so try not to let pantsing get out of control.

Ideas will pop into your head at inopportune times. A work meeting, last thing at night, in the middle of the night after you wake up because you hear a sound you don't recognise... honestly, they'll pop into your brain whenever you don't have a pen handy. So, keep a pen and paper handy, or the notes app on your phone. Always write down your ideas. You might not use them straight away, or ever, but it's so handy when you are lacking inspiration to go back through your notes and find some really good ideas! It could be an idea for a character that's been living in your head for ages, it could be a sentence you think would make an awesome opener, it could be a short description of a place you visit that struck something inside of you.

Whatever it is, it's possible material for a short romance.

Release Strategies

This is another marketing strategy.

Initially, in January 2021 (the 11th, to be precise) I decided to start spending all my time and energy on short romance. I did this with the Inner-City Alphas. Raife, Shane, Locke and Nathan all took a week each to write, format and get up for pre-order. By the time I was writing Flint, I felt my love for the series (and Alpha men) waning. I re-wrote Flint several times (pantsing my way into tangents that didn't work), which in turn ate into the space I had between finishing a book and releasing a book. By the time I was writing Colt, I was exhausted with the series, exhausted with writing, and just plain sick of it.

Colt was literally ready the day before it was released...and it cost me.

My pre-orders for the Alpha Bodyguard series took a massive hit.

I was still releasing weekly but now I was constantly against the wall. I managed to pull off Her Brazen, Beast, Back-Up and Brave Bodyguards weekly, but it took ages for me to get Burly done and released in June (four weeks late!)

So, I took a break, because I was experiencing all the symptoms of burn out.

I didn't start writing again until August of that year. That is a huge gap (seven weeks), in the realm of Short Romance. The readership I had initially built quite quickly had all but disappeared and it was like starting over.

But then I found a flow that worked for me.

And that flow is different for everyone.

There are authors who find it within themselves to write and release weekly for months at a time (like six plus months of weekly releases...) then there are those of us who sometimes struggle to release monthly depending on the other factors happening in our lives.

I would suggest you write as many books as you can before you begin releasing so you can figure out a schedule that works for you, your readers, and your bank account.

Write in advance and try to get ahead of yourself. Again, this will be a brain/personality thing, so if you find it doesn't work for you – it's okay. Find what does work and use it to your advantage as much as you can.

Some writers believe that you can train your readers. I'm not sure about this as it isn't something I've looked into too deeply. Essentially, if you release every two weeks, your readers will become accustomed to getting a new hit of dopamine every two weeks when your new release drops.

The weekly release argument is more to do with algorithms which is far and above anything I understand. But I will say from my experience, whenever I release weekly, Amazon pushes my books in front of people.

Newsletters

This is the final Marketing strategy I will talk about in this book.

This is something I fought against for a long time because I thought the following;

> *No one wants to read what I have to natter about.*
>
> *No one will buy if I put a link to my books in a newsletter because it's like cold calling.*
>
> *No one will subscribe to my email list.*
>
> *I don't have time to waste if people aren't going to read it anyway.*

I was wrong.

I was so so so so so so wrong!

I finally started a newsletter in July (maybe June) of 2022 and holy moly the difference is HUGE. People **do** read. They even reply!!! They **do** click the links; they **do** buy the books I put in there. *They join because they want to read what I have to say.* And your readers will be the same.

It's amazing and I was so stupid not to do it sooner.

I would suggest getting your newsletter set up with

a welcome automation BEFORE YOU RELEASE ANY BOOKS.

I mean, you do you by all means.

BUT if it's one thing I regret, it's not having the newsletter sooner.

I now write to my subscribers three times a week. **Three.**

I've gone from, 'Maybe I'll write them once a month, just a paragraph or so,' to, 'I'm'a write you three times a week and if you don't like it, unsubscribe.'

I tend to write an introductory paragraph of randomness, then I'll add buttons that lead to any freebies (via bookfunnel) and then I'll add one of my books to the bottom with a link to buy and a link to review.

Honestly, it has been game changing.

Once you've got yourself a newsletter set up with a small amount of subscribers you can start taking part in newsletter swaps and collaborations. Which only serves to HELP when it comes to selling your stories.

An example of how I write a Short Romance.

Note: I write using duel Points Of View in first person present tense. The story is happening NOW and you get to see both sides. Obviously, if you're writing same-sex romance, you would change accordingly.

Most Short Romance is written in this style, but if you prefer any other combination of points of view and tense and styles, go for it.

Generally, in romance, you'll get the points of view of either of the main characters or both. And in Short Romance, there is no room for other POV's to be popping up.

Prologue

This is a few paragraphs at best and I only use a prologue if I need to introduce some back story or a POV from a character other than the main characters. Otherwise, I'll just jump in straight at Chapter One with whichever POV I want to start with and use the prologue words elsewhere.

An example of this is Bea's POV in the Secret Cupid Series. She introduces whom she is going to matchmake, introducing the reader to the trope (matchmaking, mountain man and curvy young woman) and the names of each character but not much else.

Chapter One – Intro To FMC And MMC

You can write whichever you want first, but then that will generally be the way it stays in every chapter. I use their names as subheadings so the reader knows whose POV they are reading.

It will look like this.

Chapter One

Annika

It's freezing cold today. I briefly wonder why I chose to move to the mountains when I glance out of the bedroom window and immediately remember. Solitude. Glorious, wonderful solitude.

Brian

The snow is coming down heavier by the second as I eagerly await the arrival of the last hikers. I hope they haven't been slowed down for any reason other than the weather. The hot prickle of worry scrapes the back of my neck as I wonder if they've injured themselves, or worse, left the trail.

Chapter Two – Meet Cute

Again, from each of their perspectives. I usually do one, and then I'll go back in time, so we see the first character from the second's point of view for the first time. This is a style choice—you don't have to do it that way.

It's all those first-time feels that readers love. You can also use this time to describe your characters from the other's perspective. Use this to tell the reader about the initial attraction, the thing that draws the two characters together. (This will depend on tropes – falling in love with brother's best friend, new job – boss, someone saving you etc.)

Does he love the way she wears her hair?

Does she love the way his eyes burn her skin?

Chapter Three – Getting To Know Each Other, First Kiss/Clear Desire

Here we need to see them falling for each other. So naturally, they need to be spending time together, this is where you can expand on your tropes which came into play in the meet cute. Forced proximity, mistaken identity at a bar, blind date, did one rescue the other etc.

And then... **the first kiss.**

The first kiss doesn't have to happen here. But I always think it's a good catalyst for panic to set in and all the conflicting feelings to rear their ugly heads.

'I've only just met this man, what am I doing? How am I feeling such strong and crazy feelings?'

'This woman is driving me wild, and I've only just scratched the surface. How does she do this to me?'

If you're writing squeaky-clean romance, this is where those sparks fly where the characters are showing their clear desire for one another within their limits. They don't have to kiss to get the feels across. There are so many stages of intimacy you could use instead. Maybe it's a look that passes between them. Loads of internal dialogue with conflict and angst and body language. That can be just as soul-searing as any kiss. Especially if it reminds the reader of the first time they ever felt those feelings.

If you do write the kiss, it has to be the kind of kiss that could end the world.

Chapter Four – Internal Conflict

This can come because they shared a kiss they didn't expect to set them on fire. Or it can come before they kiss and realise despite conflict and doubt, they do have a real attraction to each other, but maybe they shouldn't be having that attraction to each other. Maybe one of them is from the wrong side of the track or they don't portray the person that the character's parents want them to be with.

So. Much. Conflict. All internal.

You could even introduce a couple of side characters here and this can all be a conversation. But add in the internal stuff too as it gives us a glimpse of who this character really is and where their head is at. The side characters can then be used in later romances.

Chapter Five – Intimacy And Falling In Love

If you are writing clean romance, this is where you would do all the intimate stuff, the light brushing of fingertips over bare skin (like an arm, keep it clean), the glances, eyes meeting and darting away, the sharing of something important and personal, and then a kiss. Chaste and light, but inside they are screaming that they will marry this person before they spontaneously combust with love and desire. This is the moment that they *know* this is the person for them.

If you are writing steamy romance, then this is the sex scene. Whatever level of steam you choose to write, keep it the same across the series. You'll find readers will have a certain scope of steam they'll read, and they won't like it if you start off with light steam and then give them full-blown erotica by the last book.

After this intimate time, clean or steamy, they both need to have the realisation that they are falling in love.

This can be shown as part of the same scene, or a following scene which can be from the other's point of view or even another chapter.

Chapter Six – Dark Moment

Here something happens to cause a misunderstanding or for one of their insecurities to rise up and cause trouble. Or an ex! Exes can be dastardly in a short romance. This is what I used in Raife. But briefly. The ex makes a play for Harriet and Raife goes full Alpha on him. Some readers don't like "Other Man/Other Woman" drama. In this instance, I would mention it in the blurb so the reader is aware of what they are purchasing.

At least one of them has to come to the realisation that they can't be together, and they need to tell the other one this.

This is the dark moment. Character one is heartbroken that they can't be with character two for whatever reason and character two doesn't fully understand character one's reasoning at all.

They part and try to live their lives as normally as possible. Only nothing is normal anymore. How could it be? They are twin flames, they are soul mates. They feel utterly dreadful without having the other in their life, but they try to move on through the physical and emotional pain.

Chapter Seven - Resolution

Something has to happen to bring them together. A stern talking to from a friend or family member, an accident where their life flashes before them and they realise it's no life at all without the other person in it. This is then the declaration of love moment. When the clouds part and the sunshine burns away all the negativity of the misunderstanding/reason. Either character one makes a massive apology or character two proves to character one they are wrong, and they belong together despite their differences or any other reason.

Chapter Eight – Happily Ever After

Your happily ever after needs to make the readers swoon. Generally, it will be an engagement, wedding or pregnancy but whichever it is, it has to be epic.

In the interest of being transparent, I do this wrong (almost two years of learning and thirty-something books it took me to realise this) I tend to make my big gooey bit the Epilogue.

But they should have the big gooey bit before the Epilogue if we're being honest. Well, that's the general consensus, by all means, write it your way!

Her Beast Bodyguard is an example of doing it wrong. It ends on a cliffhanger. Some people will argue against cliffhangers altogether, some will argue that cliffhangers keep readers reading even if it annoys them! I'm not going to tell you which way to go.

Anyway, Beast ends on a cliffhanger and then picks up MONTHS LATER with the couple on their honeymoon...

Just. No. Again, this is where you can learn from my mistakes. Her Beast Bodyguard has my most favourite characters of all (not your typical great-looking guy, and a super strong woman who can be vulnerable when she is with him), but it remains one of my lowest-read and lowest-rated books.

Also, I have started to make my gooey endings a little bit *out there*. In Tilly's Mountain Hero (spoiler alert) she gives birth to their first child on the page, introducing the couple from the next book who just so happen to be a midwife and a doctor. I thought readers would hate this. I mean; there's nothing sexy about labour and delivery. But so far, the reviews have been awesome, some singling out the epilogue as wonderful and amazing. Which warms my heart because I really enjoyed writing that scene.

Points to take away, the gooey forever in love scene has to happen in the last full chapter of your short romance.

Epilogue

The epilogue is largely used in short romance (as of the time of writing) to introduce the characters you will be focusing on in the next book in the series. It needs to show us the couple later on in time, so it could be a pregnancy announcement, a gender reveal party or something that happens chronologically after whatever happened in the last chapter. But it also needs to include at least one of the characters from the next story, or from one of the spin-offs from the story. In Bette's Mountain Hero I introduce Abbie in the story, and then in the Epilogue she is there again where I show she is pregnant with a rainbow baby. This has set the groundwork for Abbie's story which was going to be a spin-off focusing on the Rangers who work on Montrossi Ridge. However, as is my prerogative, I've decided to make Abbie a mountain rescue character now so who knows what will happen.

If you are writing the last book in the series, then you could use the space to introduce your next series (spin-off series) or you could give the readers a scene of all the characters together (this especially works if it is a family of brothers for example). As a reader I can tell you how much I LOVE this. I want to see everyone again with all their kids and pets and just the sheer amount of love shared. But, if you do this, remember that it will be very hard to break back into that series if you suddenly want to add more books to it.

Backmatter

You're allowed ten per cent of your book's content to be backmatter. That sounds like a lot (to me at least) but if you're writing a 10k-word book, that's only 1k words. I usually put the first chapter of my next-in-series book here, as previously mentioned, with a link to buy before it and after it. It looks a bit like this.

Did you enjoy Book A? Book B is available for free in KU or buy for 2.99! (this is a link)

Book B Chapter One text.

You can buy Book B for 2.99 or read for free in KU! (this is a link)

Then I put a link to join my newsletter, Facebook page, Goodreads profile, and Amazon page.

The most basic point of having back matter is the call to action. The rest is there to try and get lucky. The general consensus here is that readers will do the first thing, but ignore the rest. This is generally true in my experience.

The call to action is the very first thing after the story ends. For me, it's that I want them to purchase or download the next book. That's going to make me a short-term income. Lots of writers put their newsletter link first, because it can generate long-term income.

It's up to you how you lay out your back matter, just keep in mind that it can't be more than 10 per cent of your overall word count and Amazon might not like too many links. Amazon definitely doesn't like links that link to other marketplaces like Apple or Kobo etc. If you plan to publish wide, change your backmatter accordingly.

Finally

You've chosen to give writing short romance a try, and I'm so happy about that. Readers are finding they have less and less time to sit and enjoy a good book in their busy lives, so providing them with everything they want within a short space of time, like a lunch break, is always going to be a huge win.

There are so many resources that will be of huge benefit to you, including Facebook groups and podcasts, just do a search for instalove and indie publishing and absorb as much information as you can.

Give the instructions in this book a go and let me know how it goes. You can email me directly at nell@nellalexanderauthor.co.uk or even join my Facebook group just for readers of this book https://www.facebook.com/NellAlexanderAuthor where I can answer any questions or expand on the info I've given you.

Other Authors I have mentioned in this book:

Zoe York

Becca Syme

Gwen Hayes

Check out their amazon pages for amazing writing resources.

And last but not least, Thank You. Thank you for reading this book, thank you for considering writing Short Romance, and thank you for being awesome!

About The Author

Nell...

...has been writing instalove Short Romances since January 2021 and now has over thirty books in the genre along with ghostwriting Short Romance for other authors.
When she is not writing she can be found spending time with her family and enjoying the simple pleasures in life (which is code for wine.)

Made in United States
Troutdale, OR
03/14/2024